About the Author

Tim Cornish graduated from the London School of Economics with an honours degree in economics and later obtained an MBA from Bradford University. His early career was spent in business, in the UK and in both the Middle and the Far East.

For more than 25 years now he has worked in the UK as a consultant in the legal sector, during which time he has seen many changes in the law and in society generally, regarding the elderly.

These changes have been brought about by many factors, but chiefly the increase in longevity in the population with all the attendant benefits, and problems, which that has brought. Hand in hand with this increase in life expectancy has been an increase in the overall wealth of the populace, together with ever increasing costs, for individuals, families, and the community generally of caring for the elderly.

All these changes have resulted in new legislation, new attitudes to the elderly, new institutions, new legal and financial practices - for those concerned and for their families. It is this need to become aware of the total situation which was behind the decision to write **Life**Holder.

www.fast-print.net/store.php

Life Holder
Copyright © Tim Cornish 2013

ISBN 978-178035-538-2

First published 2013 by
FASTPRINT PUBLISHING
Peterborough, England.

An environmentally friendly book printed and bound in England by
www.printondemand-worldwide.com

Mixed Sources
Product group from well-managed
forests, and other controlled sources
FSC www.fsc.org Cert no. TT-COC-002641
© 1996 Forest Stewardship Council

PEFC Certified
This product is
from sustainably
managed forests
and controlled
sources
PEFC
www.pefc.org
PEFC/16-33-415

This book is made entirely of chain-of-custody materials

Preface

This book is called **LifeHolder** because it's about the life you hold - your own.

It's about helping you plan for your later life, so that you can best enjoy the years of retirement.

It's about helping you plan for the inevitable end of life and helping you cope with what may be a considerable prior period when you may need the help of those close to you, as well perhaps of others too.

It's about the certainty of death and the probability of prior incapacity of some degree prior to that, since medical science has become so adept at prolonging our lives and postponing eventual death.

As human beings we have a tendency to avoid thinking about difficult issues, often preferring to put them off until tomorrow, and repeating that postponement again and again, sometimes until it is too late.

The purpose of this book is to help you overcome that natural reluctance, to encourage you to consider and then to act, so that you will enjoy the peace of mind of knowing that you will have done the best for yourself and the best for those whom you care most about.

Contents

Introduction

LifeHolder has been written for the layman, as a convenient guide to those personal matters which should be contemplated and considered in middle and later life.

Much as we might not like to think about it we are all, one day, going to die. Most of us will leave behind friends, family and assets.

As we all know intrinsically, the way to deal with these issues is to make a **Will**.

A few of us also give thought to how we want our body disposed of and how we would like our passing to be marked, by making a **Funeral Plan**.

Some of us also contemplate how our death might help others live by registering our wish for **Organ** or **Tissue Donation**. And a very small number of us consider **Body Donation** for teaching or medical research so that future generations may benefit.

As medical science advances and increases our life expectancies many of us will, sadly, at some stage lose mental or physical capacity. These situations can be mitigated, to the benefit of family, friends, carers and medical staff as well as to ourselves if we consider, in advance, instruments such as **Lasting Powers of Attorney** and **Living Wills**.

Financial matters should also concern us as we approach retirement and old age. Most of us will wish to maximise the net wealth we leave behind, whether that is to benefit our children, friends, or favourite charities. This may require **Tax and Estate Planning**.

Many of us may end up with inadequate income to fund our lifestyles and will need to look at sources of finance such as **Equity Release**.

A significant, and increasing, proportion of us can contemplate needing some form of **Residential Care** in the last part of our lives. All of us need to look at the cost of such care and the effect it will have financially and emotionally on our families.

LifeHolder deals simply and briefly with all of these issues and others, not in a technical or detailed way, but in a way which raises awareness and which, hopefully, will prompt readers to seek the necessary professional advice in their own, and their families' interests.

Part A - Planning for the Inevitable

In this section we look at death and how to plan for its consequences. In particular, we look at how to minimise the distress and discomfort of relatives and friends by making a **Will**, and how **Will Registration** can help avoid the potential problem of 'missing Wills'.

We also look at the importance of **Funeral Planning** and consider the issues and practicalities of **Organ** and **Body Donation**.

1. Making a Will

The cornerstone of planning for death is making a Will. Statistics show that only some 30% of the UK population get round to taking the necessary action – so that in 7 out of 10 deaths no express wishes have been recorded by the deceased – causing distress, often disharmony, and worry to those left behind.

Why you should make a Will

If you die without making a Will the law will decide how your estate is distributed, in accordance with long established statutory intestacy rules. These rules are very unlikely to coincide with your own wishes. So there are a number of very good reasons for making a Will:

- You retain control by planning ahead
- You get to choose who receives what, not someone else
- You can provide for your loved ones
- You can mitigate the tax payable on your estate
- You can minimise the distress of those you leave behind
- You can choose your own executor(s)

Dying intestate invariably causes problems for the family, particularly where the deceased had been married more than once and there are children and/or stepchildren from more than one of those relationships. The intestacy rules are simply unable to cope adequately with that type of circumstance.

The notes below have been designed to offer some initial guidance so that you can consider the most important aspects of making a Will, collect your thoughts, and perhaps discuss the issues with your family.

This process will result in a reasonably clear idea of what you want to do. It will facilitate discussion with your solicitor, who will be able to help fill in the details and offer the most practical advice on how your wishes can be accommodated, in the most convenient, straightforward and cost-efficient way.

Matters for Consideration

The following are important matters you should give thought to:

a) Children
If you have young children (under the age of 18) your surviving spouse or partner will probably continue to care for them. However you should consider appointing guardians in the event you and your spouse die at the same time – it can happen! This will require some deep thought and discussion with the person or persons you want to appoint, so that everyone feels comfortable about the arrangement. You may also want to provide for monies to be invested until your children reach the age of 18 (or older, if you wish). If you have a child which is disadvantaged or disabled you will be particularly concerned to make adequate arrangements for their welfare and well-being after your death.

b) Inheritance Tax & Estate Planning
You do not have to be very wealthy to be caught in the inheritance tax net. With the majority of people now owning their own home, and with the value of those homes in many cases exceeding the tax threshold, many estates will attract IHT.

However, there are a number of legitimate means to avoid or mitigate the effect of this tax. Your solicitor can advise you on these and help you choose the most effective means to suit your circumstances.

c) Executors

An executor is someone, nominated by the person making the Will, who will have the responsibility of administering the estate after death. You need to decide who you wish to deal with your estate and carry out the instructions specified in your Will. This should be someone who knows you and whom you can trust. (You can nominate someone who is also a beneficiary of your Will if you wish.)

Because some estates can prove to be quite complicated, many people choose to appoint a professional person, such as a solicitor, as a joint (or sole) executor. This is a safeguard and can be useful where your other chosen executor is a lay person. You should note, however, that a professional person so appointed will make a charge for their services in this regard.

d) Assets & Liabilities

In order to draw up your Will you will need to consider what you will leave behind (referred to as your estate).

You should draw up an initial list of all your assets – these include your house, your investments and savings including any shares you hold, bank accounts, insurance policies and pension funds as well as family heirlooms, antiques etc.

There may be liabilities which you currently have, such as a mortgage. These need to be totalled and the amount deducted from assets to give a figure for your approximate net assets. A precise valuation is not required but your solicitor will need to know the general order so they can advise on minimising any tax liabilities your estate may attract.

e) Your Wishes

Sometimes the most difficult part of the exercise is to decide how you want your estate to be distributed after your death. Possible beneficiaries include your spouse, your children, your grandchildren, any siblings, nephews and nieces.

In addition to family you may also wish to leave legacies to godchildren, friends, charities or other bodies.

If you have been married more than once and if you have children from one or more of the marriages you will need to consider how you wish to have them benefit from your estate. The situation is further complicated if your spouse or partner also has children from a previous marriage, and will need discussion between all parties.

You also need to consider how you want the beneficiaries to benefit –via specified amounts (e.g. £1000) or by proportion (e.g. half of my estate) or via specific item (e.g. my wristwatch to my grandson). In almost all instances there is a residue after the specific bequests have been made. Whom do you wish to receive this residue?

Remember there is always the possibility that one or more of your beneficiaries may die before you. You should therefore give some thought to alternatives.

Reviewing Your Will

You should note that it is very important to review your Will from time to time, every few years at least.

Your circumstances may change, your family and friends may grow or contract, or the law may change in a way which requires changes to your arrangements to ensure they remain tax efficient and correspond with your wishes.

A Note on Ownership of Foreign Property

Increasing numbers of us are realising their dreams by investing in foreign property, either to have a holiday home in the sun or as an eventual retirement home.

However, most foreign countries have succession laws which are very different from our own, a fact which makes it difficult in all cases (and impossible in most) to deal with the eventual disposal of the property in a Will drawn up under English law.

The issue can be quite complex and requires legal advice. You should seek professional advice to deal with this issue if you have, or are contemplating purchasing, a property overseas.

2. Registering Your Will

It is a sad fact that, every year, a proportion of those who die having made a Will, in fact die intestate. This is because their Will is never found.

It is traditional in the UK for solicitors to retain the original copy of each Will they draw up on behalf of their clients – the vast majority of firms offer this as a free service. However, although Wills may be safely and securely stored in this way, they can only be used for the purpose intended, if the solicitor concerned is informed that the person has died!

Sadly, in a significant number of deaths each year, the family and friends of the deceased are unaware of the existence or location of a Will. The result is that the Will may not be found, with the consequence that the estate has to be wound up (and distributed) according to the rules of intestacy. This means that the testator's wishes, as expressed in the Will, will not be carried out. Family, friends, charities, and other potential beneficiaries may not then receive the inheritances that the testator wished them to have.

Fortunately there is now a national Will Register which can help ensure that Wills are found after the testator dies.

The Will Register is called Certainty and can be found at www.certainty.co.uk. Registration can be done simply and quickly for a small one-off fee, either by the solicitor acting for the testator, or the testator themselves.

Only the name of the testator, the date of the Will, and the location of the original Will are required for registration. The relationship between solicitor and testator and the contents of the Will itself remain confidential, but the register can be searched by someone seeking the whereabouts of a Will after the death of the testator.

Anyone who then approaches the solicitor holding the Will would have to demonstrate their credentials and their right to have possession of the document, in the normal way.

3. Types of Funeral

Not knowing what the deceased would have wanted; in respect of the funeral service (music, readings, hymns etc.); in respect of disposal of the body (burial or cremation); and sometimes whether or not they would have wanted to donate any of their organs can cause the greatest anguish and worry to those left behind.

This section considers the topic of funeral planning, and the importance of making your family aware of your wishes.

a) "Conventional" Funerals
The vast majority of funerals in the UK are conducted with some form of religious ceremony and about 70% are cremations, with most of the remainder being burials.

b) Non-Religious Funerals
However, for those who have lived their life without religion it is possible to have a non-religious ceremony. The British Humanist Association (www.humanism.org.uk) offers a service whereby a trained officiant will conduct a non-religious ceremony celebrating the life of the deceased.

As to the disposal of the body, if cremation or burial in a churchyard or local authority graveyard is not what you want there are a couple of alternatives.

c) Burial at Sea
It is possible to be buried at sea, although this is discouraged by the authorities – there are three licensed locations in the UK; off Newhaven, Sussex or The Needles, Isle of Wight, or Tynemouth, Northumbria. Just 50 or so non-navy burials at sea are granted each year by the Marine Management Organisation, to whom application has to be made.

An embalmed body cannot be buried at sea (embalming chemicals might, over time, contaminate the water). Therefore if this is an option you want you should make sure that family members are aware of your wishes so that undertakers do not embalm your body.

d) Burial in non-consecrated ground

A second alternative to a cremation or burial in a cemetery is burial in non-consecrated ground. Such burials have long been possible and there are now around 200 woodland burial sites in the UK which offer this alternative to cemeteries. These are managed privately (often by farmers) or by a local authority.

There are no gravestones or other signs or monuments. Burial sites are either left unmarked, or are marked by the planting of a tree or wild flowers.

As in burial at sea, the body must not be embalmed, in order to prevent possible contamination of the watercourse. Also, for such burials any coffin used must be made from a fully degradable material such as cardboard or wicker, or a cloth or drape used instead.

Further information can be found by contacting The Natural Death Centre (www.naturaldeath.org.uk) or telephone 01962 712690.

4. Advance Funeral Directives

To ensure you have the funeral ceremony which you want, with the music, poems, readings etc. of your choice you need to make your immediate family aware, so that they can begin to carry out your wishes immediately, before any irreversible actions may be taken.

The best way of ensuring your wishes are carried out is to make an Advance Funeral Wish or Directive. Making such a directive means that you decide and those who you leave behind are spared the (sometimes difficult) decisions, and having to guess what you might have wanted.

The Directive can be a fairly simple document stating your preference as to cremation or burial and perhaps nominating the hymns or other music you would like played. However, it can be as comprehensive as you like and go down to such details as to who you want to be bearers of your coffin, where and how you would like the news of your death to be announced, and so on.

A downloadable, very detailed format, of an Advance Funeral Directive can be downloaded, free of charge, from the Bereavement Advice Centre at www.bereavementadvice.org

If you do make an Advance Funeral Directive the key thing is to let your near family know that you have and where it is located so it is accessed quickly after death, thereby allowing your wishes to be carried out.

5. Organ & Tissue Donation

Every year around 400 people die in the UK while waiting for a lung, liver, kidney or heart transplant. If you wish to help reduce that statistic you may like to consider becoming an organ donor.

There is a critical shortage of organs and the gap between the number of organs donated and the number of people waiting for a transplant is increasing. According to NHS statistics, at any time more than 7000 people in the UK need an organ transplant. It is a paradox that as medical science advances and makes more transplants possible, with increasing chances of success, the gap grows.

Organs that can be donated after death include the heart, lungs, kidneys, liver, pancreas and small bowel. Tissues such as skin, bone, heart valves and corneas can also be used to help others.

Eligibility for donation

Virtually anyone can elect, and be accepted, to be a donor.

Age is not a barrier. In the case of cornea and some other tissue age is not a factor at all. For other transplants it is the person's physical condition which is the crucial factor. Successful transplants have been achieved from donors in their 70's and 80's.

Ethnicity is not a barrier. On the contrary the more diverse the backgrounds of potential donors on the Register the better, since organs are matched by blood group and tissue type, meaning that patients from the same ethnic group are more likely to make a close match.

Even potential donors with an existing medical condition can be accepted. A decision about whether particular organs are suitable is made, at the time of death, by doctors taking account of the person's medical history. In most cases it is possible for some organs to be donated.

None of the major religions in the UK object to the concept of organ or tissue donation. However, if you are in any doubt you should discuss the matter with your spiritual or religious adviser.

Becoming a Donor

The NHS operates an Organ Donor Register which over 17 million people have already joined. This is an entirely confidential database of those who are willing to donate after their death.

You can join the Register by calling 0300 123 23 23, or visiting their website which is found at www.organdonation.nhs.uk. (Other means of registering include when applying for a driving license, when registering at a GP surgery, or when registering for a European Health Insurance Card.)

In addition to being placed on the Register you will receive a donor card which you can carry with you.

As well as potentially helping others to live or improve their lives, becoming a donor can also help your family. They may be faced with having to decide whether to accede to a request for organ or tissue donation after your death – making such a decision would be so much easier if they knew, in advance, what your wishes would be.

6. Donating your body for Medical Research or Training

Over the past few years the numbers of bodies left to medical research has been falling – to the point where many senior doctors and surgeons are becoming very concerned.

Traditionally medical students have learned their trade by dissecting human bodies – clearly a preferred route to performing surgery on a live person. The fall in numbers of bodies available for training purposes now means that some budding surgeons are unable to learn in this way. One leading surgeon recently stated he "found it worrying" that for a newly qualified surgeon their first incision would be made on a living person.

No bodies can be accepted for teaching purposes if organs have been removed for donation (except if only the corneas are to be donated). A body will also not be accepted if it has been subject to a post-mortem examination or the person had been severely deformed or suffered from hepatitis, dementia or severe obesity.

A bequest to leave your body for research or training must be made in writing in the presence of a witness. You should complete the necessary forms, available from The Human Tissue Authority.

Part B -
Potential Incapacity

Having looked at death itself we now look at the (very real) possibility that, before we die, we may suffer some serious mental or physical incapacity. Utilising a **Lasting Power of Attorney** can mitigate the distressing consequences of incapacity to the benefit of all concerned.

If incapacity occurs and no Power of Attorney has been arranged, a **Deputyship** may need to be arranged.

Unless death comes suddenly and unexpectedly there is likely to be a period of time leading up to the event when you will need medical care. You, and those treating you, may be faced with decisions about the nature of the treatment you receive. Your ability to communicate your wishes may become impaired. We look at how an **Advance Directive** (or **Living Will**) can help in such circumstances.

1. Lasting Power of Attorney

Making a Will records one's wishes in the event of death. However, circumstances may arise before death where one becomes seriously incapacitated – to the extent that mental capacity is insufficient to make considered decisions and judgements about one's own affairs.

Commonly, diseases such as Alzheimer's and other forms of dementia overtake elderly people. But other conditions such as motor neurone disease, or indeed unexpected traumas such as accidents, can affect us at any age.

In such circumstances, where we become unable to manage our own affairs, the law adopts a "protective stance". It permits no-one, not even our spouse or other near relative, access to our bank account or other financial assets, without due process. That process is through the aptly named Court of Protection and involves the appointment of a Deputy. The problem is that the process is costly and protracted and, until settled, there are bills to be paid and decisions which cannot be made (see below under Deputyship).

All of this can cause stress and inconvenience, to all concerned.

Fortunately there is a legal device which, if in place at the time incapacity occurs, will minimise the delay and avoid application to the Court. This device is known as a Lasting Power of Attorney (LPA).

Purpose of an LPA

An LPA is a legal document which enables you, in advance of any potential incapacity, to nominate one or more people (attorneys) to deal with your affairs, on your behalf, should you become prevented from doing so yourself by mental illness or disability.

The vital requirement is to anticipate the possibility of future mental incapacity and draw up the document *before* such incapacity occurs. It is not possible to appoint an attorney after the event.

For most of us it is impossible to anticipate if or when we might succumb to mental incapacity. It is therefore prudent, particularly so when we are in middle age and therefore closer to the possibility, to set up an LPA.

There are two types of LPA – one deals with Personal Welfare and the other deals with Property & Affairs.

Lasting Power of Attorney – Personal Welfare (LPA Welfare)

This allows you to appoint one or more attorneys to take decisions about your healthcare and general welfare should you lose the capacity to do so yourself.

You can specify restrictions or conditions on the decisions they may make, or you can give them general power to make any decision they may consider necessary. If you wish you can give them authority to give or refuse consent to life-sustaining treatment on your behalf.

Lasting Power of Attorney – Property & Affairs (LPA Finance)

This allows you to appoint one or more attorneys to take decisions about your property and financial affairs should you lose the capacity to do so yourself.

As with the Personal Welfare LPA you can specify any restrictions or conditions you wish, or you can give them general authority to deal with your affairs.

Benefits of an LPA

An LPA has a number of advantages; it enables you to retain control of your affairs (by proxy), it helps guarantee your future security and it can relieve your family/friends of distress and worry.

By setting up an LPA you can create a framework that will allow your affairs to be administered by someone of your own choosing who you know and trust, should you be prevented from acting on your own behalf sometime in the future.In the event you are rendered incapable of administering your own affairs, and you have not set up an LPA (Finance), your estate and your financial affairs will be managed by the Court of Protection who will arrange for a Deputy to be appointed.

If you have not set up an LPA (Welfare) decisions about your health and welfare will be taken by doctors and medical staff, social workers, carers and others in whose care you might be. If you are incapable of communicating your wishes you will have no control over any decisions they may take.

Setting up an LPA

This must be done by completing a statutory form (a separate form for each type of LPA). Although you can do it yourself, the form and procedures concerned are quite complex and many people prefer to have the benefit of professional advice and help.

Firstly, you need to consider whether or not you wish to set up both types of LPA, or whether you prefer to make arrangements for just one of the different types of issues. You may wish to discuss this with family and friends.

Appointing Attorneys

Secondly, you need to consider who you want to appoint as your attorney or whether you would like to have two or more joint attorneys. Whoever you appoint they should be someone you can trust implicitly. Usually this means a very close relative or, if that is not possible, a professional person such as a solicitor.

If you decide to set up both types of LPA you can, if you wish, appoint different attorneys for each type. It may well be, for example, that someone you think suitable to act on your behalf on health and welfare issues would not be suitable to deal with your financial affairs, or vice versa. If this is the case you will need different attorneys for each LPA.

You then need to think about what powers you want to give your attorney(s). You can, as noted above, give general powers or very limited and specific ones.

Whilst virtually anyone over the age of 18 (provided they are not bankrupt) can be appointed as an attorney, in practice most will be close family members or professional advisers since they should be people you can trust implicitly.

Certificate Provider

In order to prevent fraud and to deter potential abuse of powers it is a requirement of the legislation governing LPAs that an independent person* discusses with you your intent to establish an LPA. This person, if satisfied that you understand the purpose of the LPA and that you are not being coerced or pressured to sign the form, then signs the part of the form entitled "Statement of certificate provider". Without such a signature the form will not be valid and the LPA will not be granted.

The independent person can be someone who is known to you, but cannot be a relative, or your spouse or civil partner; neither can he or she be a nominated attorney, or a current paid carer, or a manager or employee of any care home where you reside, or someone named on the form as a person to be notified of the registration of the LPA. If there is no-one who you know personally outside of these categories you can discuss your intent to set up the LPA with a solicitor, barrister, bank manager, clergyman, or other professional person.

Registering an LPA

An LPA, before it becomes effective, has to be registered with the Office of the Public Guardian. This will take 11 or 12 weeks to complete but, provided application is made in good time, the LPA will be 'in place' and can be effected immediately incapacity becomes evident.

2. Deputyship

As noted above, if a person becomes incapable of handling their own affairs through some sort of incapacity, someone else has to take over.

If forethought has been applied and an attorney appointed under an LPA, that attorney can (provided the LPA has been registered, as described above) immediately begin to handle the person's affairs, according to the powers given to them in the document.

By contrast, if no LPA had been established prior to the onset of incapacity, a Deputy has to be appointed by the Court of Protection to manage the affairs of the person concerned.

Dealing with the Court can be time consuming and complex – and costly. Appointment of a Deputy can take many weeks, and the person eventually appointed may be someone not even known to the incapacitated person.

The Court will determine the powers that the Deputy has in acting on the person's behalf and will grant them responsibility for property and financial affairs including maintaining a bank account, paying bills, purchasing property, and arranging finances generally. The Deputy will have to account to the Court on an annual basis. The Court will supervise the Deputy in their duties throughout the duration of the deputyship to the degree commensurate with the Court's view of their competence and experience.

Setting up an LPA has its costs, including the cost of professional advice and Court fees.

However, appointing a Deputy will undoubtedly incur larger (and ongoing) fees.

The decision, eventually for all of us, is whether to incur the relatively low costs of setting up a Lasting Power of Attorney *before the possibility* of incapacity, or taking the risk that incapacity will not affect us before death and that the protracted, complex and more expensive costs of having the Court of Protection appoint a Deputy (with consequent distress and inconvenience to our family) will be avoided.

3. Advance Directive (Living Will)

An Advance Directive (or Living Will) is a document which tells your doctors what kind of medical care you would like if you become unable to make decisions on your own behalf or unable to communicate your wishes.

A Lasting Power of Attorney – Personal Welfare enables you to appoint an attorney or attorneys to act on your behalf in health and welfare matters. A Living Will provides an alternative means for you to determine the medical treatment you wish to receive if you have lost capacity to communicate with your carers.

Because a Living Will is not a statutory document and has no defined format it can be a more flexible instrument than an LPA; it can also be less expensive to draw up.

Neither document has anything to do with the distribution of your estate after death, (this is covered by your Will).

A growing number of people are choosing to make living wills because:

- You can make your own wishes clear, while you are able
- You help prevent those closest to you from having to make difficult decisions on your behalf
- You help those treating you by informing them about your wishes and absolving them from the task of guessing what you would want
- You take control of your future medical treatment

In the absence of a Living Will or an LPA, and if you are unable to communicate your wishes, your doctors will decide what treatment they think is in your best interests. Although they may consult your next of kin or immediate family, it is they who ultimately decide what to do. If you make a Living Will you can set out what medical treatment you wish to accept or refuse in such circumstances.

Living Wills and the Law

The Mental Capacity Act 2005, which became effective on 1 October 2007, has clarified the law on Advance Decisions/Living Wills and given them legal status.

Format of a Living Will

There is no statutory document or defined format for a Living Will.

It can be a fairly simple statement of your wishes, expressed in generalities rather than specifics but which, nevertheless, give the medical team treating you a good indication of your wishes. Alternatively the document can be quite detailed, specifying what you wish in different circumstances, or for different conditions or illnesses.

You may, in the document, nominate a "Health Care Proxy" (a position similar to an attorney appointed under an LPA - Personal Welfare). This would typically be a close friend or relative who knows your wishes and can communicate them to the medical team on your behalf.

The document should be signed by you, in the presence of (preferably) two witnesses not related to you and who do not expect to benefit from your death. It should also name your General Practitioner and give his or her contact details.

Once you have completed your Living Will you should ensure that all those close to you know that you have done so, and where it is located.

N.B. If you want to refuse life-sustaining treatment in your Living Will you must include a statement that your wishes apply to the specific treatment or treatments, even if your life is at risk.

Professional Advice

You should certainly consult your doctor. This will help you to know exactly what the healthcare options are and, after you have drawn up the document, you should ensure he or she has a copy and a note to the effect on your medical record.

Because the document is legally binding you should consult a solicitor to help you draw one up. They will have a number of different Living Will "formats" which can be used or adapted to suit your circumstances and to enable you to explicitly express your wishes.

Note that you can always change the wishes stated in your Living Will, at any time while you are able to communicate.

Part C -
Financial Planning

Financial planning is always important, but never more so than when contemplating your retirement old age, and death.

When drawing up your Will **Inheritance Tax and Estate Planning** needs to be addressed. After retirement you may need to look at means of supplementing your income by downsizing your home or **Releasing Equity** from it.

Perhaps you may also wish to put aside some regular savings to **Fund your Funeral** costs or for other purposes and you may also wish to consider purchasing a **Funeral Bond**.

These are mostly areas where professional advice is needed, both legal and financial, and if necessary most solicitors would expect to advise you in concert with an appropriate independent financial adviser.

1. Inheritance Tax & Estate Planning

Estate planning refers to the whole process of forward planning to ensure that what you want to occur after your death does indeed happen, and taking the right steps to ensure that tax payable on your estate (and therefore borne by your beneficiaries) is minimised. As such, estate planning includes the process of drawing up a Will, and including within that document appropriate devices to achieve your aims.

IHT is payable on any estate where the net value exceeds £325,000 (this figure will remain the same until at least 2015). The rate of tax imposed is 40% on the whole amount above the threshold (although this reduces to 36% where 10% or more of the net estate is left to charity). The inheritance tax on an estate worth £500,000 would therefore be £70,000 (40% of £175,000).

When it is due IHT must be paid before probate is granted – that is, before any monies left in the Will can be distributed.

Marriage & Civil Partnership

Assets which pass from one spouse or civil partner to another are exempt from the tax. So if on death, someone leaves everything they own to their spouse or civil partner, it is exempt from IHT and they have not used any of their nil rate band.

The unused nil band rate can now be transferred to the surviving spouse or civil partner. Thus, no IHT is payable on the first death and the nil band rate on the second death will be £650,000 (2 x £325,000).

If some of the nil band rate was used on the first death, not all of the rate can be transferred. For example, if the first death occurred during 2007-08 (when the nil tax band was £300,000) and the deceased left assets worth £150,000 to the children and everything else to the spouse, one half of the nil band rate was unused and can be transferred.

If the second death occurs in 2011 (when the nil rate band is £325,000) the amount available for transfer would be 50% of £325,000, or £162,500. Therefore the tax free part of the estate of the second spouse would be £487,500 (£325,000 plus £162,500).

In contrast to people who are married or in a civil partnership, cohabiting couples cannot transfer the nil rate band on the first death. Therefore if one cohabitee leaves all their estate to the other, IHT will be payable on everything above £325,000 of the total estate on the second death (as opposed to everything above £650,000 in the case of marriage or civil partnership).

The estates of single people and divorcees will also be subject to IHT on all amounts over £325,000. For these individuals and for the very wealthy it is possible to reduce IHT liability by creating different types of trusts. Some of these are described briefly below but the legal and financial environment can be complex and is subject to change, so professional advice should always be sought. Other means of mitigating IHT include making gifts (also dealt with below).

Types of Trusts

a) Asset Preservation Trusts
protect pension death benefits from IHT, ensure that they are not assessed as capital should the surviving spouse require long-term care, and guarantee that the benefits pass to your children rather than your spouse's new husband or wife should they remarry.

b) Business Trusts
hold life assurance arrangements by Partners or Directors to allow flexibility in ownership through death or retirement, and ensure that the surviving partners/directors have the money to buy the deceased's share of the business, and ensure the deceased's beneficiaries get a fair price for the latter's share in the business.

c) Guardianship Protection Trusts
operate on a life assurance plan creating funds for guardians to look after orphaned children.

d) Gift Plan Trusts
allow investment via an Investment Bond ensuring that IHT is mitigated if the donor survives seven years since the original value of the gift (along with any growth in value) will be outside the estate.

e) Absolute Trusts
allow gifts to a grandchild (for example, for school or university fees) allowing the recipient to make use of their personal tax allowance.

f) Life Interest Trusts
where the specified beneficiary is entitled to receive for life the income generated by the trust's investments, but the capital passes (on death) to the next set of beneficiaries, for example children.

g) Inheritance Creation Trusts
operate on the basis of a life assurance plan (either single life or joint life second death) creating funds for anticipated IHT liability, so that the tax can be paid quickly, allowing the swift granting of probate. Alternatively the cash generated may be used to create an additional legacy.

Tax Exempt Gifts

Certain gifts are exempt from IHT and other taxes. These include:

- Anything you give your spouse (provided he/she lives in the UK)
- Gifts to UK charities, museums, universities, the National Trust and certain other institutions
- Gifts of up to £3,000 in any one tax year
- Gifts of up to £250 to as many people as you wish
- Wedding gifts of up to £5,000 to each of your children
- Wedding gifts of up to £2,500 to each of your grandchildren
- Wedding gifts of up to £1,000 to anyone else

Larger Transfers of Capital

HM Revenue & Customs will permit the transfer of limitless sums to UK based individuals. Such transfers are known as Potentially Exempt Transfers (PETS). "Potentially" since they escape IHT entirely provided the donor survives for seven years.

If the donor dies at any time within the seven years tax will be payable on a sliding scale – for example, if death occurs between 3 and 4 years after donation tax will be levied at 80% of the standard rate, if it occurs between 4 and 5 years after donation the rate falls to 60% of the standard rate, and so on.

Clearly it is best, from the tax point of view, if such transfers are made as early in life as possible. However, you must be at a stage in life when you can reasonably judge how much you can afford to give away without depriving yourself of the lifestyle you would like!

2. Equity Release

Millions of elderly and retired people are living in homes whose values have greatly appreciated in recent years but are struggling on limited pensions – they are asset-rich but cash-poor.

Equity Release schemes allow you to borrow money from a financial institution against the value of your home. The loan is paid off on your death, or the death of your surviving spouse or when the latter moves into a care home. You keep the right to live in your home for the rest of your life. The money raised can be used in any way you wish.

To qualify for a scheme the youngest occupant normally has to be at least 65 (although some institutions go as low as 55) and the property needs to be freehold or have at least 75 years of a lease remaining.

There are two main types of scheme – Lifetime Mortgage and Home Reversion. Each has advantages and disadvantages.

Lifetime Mortgages

With this type of scheme you borrow money from a financial institution and give the lender a mortgage over your home. The loan can be either rolled-up interest or interest only. Typically you would be able to borrow anything from 18% to 50% of the value of the property, depending or your age and that of your partner.

a) Rolled-up Interest loan

Here you raise a lump sum but make no monthly payments. Instead the interest is added each month to the amount borrowed. The interest builds up year after year (hence "rolled-up") and is paid off, along with the original loan, when your home is eventually sold.

This type of scheme is risky because the amount you owe can mount up very quickly. If the loan runs for a long time you could end up owing more than the house is worth. It is therefore important to look for a "no negative equity" guarantee with this type of scheme.

Of course, the longer the loan runs the less your family will receive in inheritance after your death.

b) Interest-Only Loan

With interest-only schemes the amount you owe does not increase over the years so there is no possibility of running down the value of your family's inheritance. The disadvantage, however, is that you do have to make monthly payments of interest for the rest of your life.

Such a scheme could therefore be of interest to those who want to raise a capital sum for some purpose where there is already an adequate income stream coming into the household.

c) Drawdown or Flexible Loans
Some providers now provide the option of allowing partial drawdowns of the total mortgage agreed, as cash is required. By not withdrawing the total amount at commencement the borrower saves on interest payments.

Home Reversion Plans

With a reversion plan you sell all or part of your home to an investment company in exchange for a guarantee that you continue to live in the property as a tenant (rent free or for a nominal rent) for the rest of your life, plus a tax-free lump sum.

You will not receive the full market value for the property (or part thereof) but a percentage of it according to your age and gender.

When the property is sold on your death the investment company receives a share of the proceeds, corresponding to the percentage share they originally purchased. The balance will go to your estate.

Other Options

By far the easiest, and cheapest, way to release equity is to sell your home and buy a cheaper one.

This can often be achieved practically as you may not need a large house (or garden) in your later years and can downsize while retaining the standard of accommodation you are used to.

Other options might include renting out part of the house, although the consequent lack of privacy would be a disadvantage.

Finally, if your children (the eventual beneficiaries) are in a position to do so they might step in and help you out financially, thus protecting their inheritance and enabling you to remain in your home.

Further Information

Equity release requires a good deal of thought and consideration. The notes above are intended only as a short introductory guide to the subject.

As Help the Aged has said "Before you take out any scheme of this type, it is vital that you seek independent financial and legal advice".

3. Long-Term Residential Care

The possibility of moving into a long-term residential care home is one which potentially faces us all.

Local Authority or NHS Funding?

When you go into a care home for 'social' rather than 'health' reasons it is the local authority, not the NHS, which is the 'controlling' authority and it is they who will determine whether you will be asked to contribute towards the costs, and if so, by how much.

Please note that if care is required primarily for health reasons it is the NHS which is the funding authority, not the local authority – this section deals only with local authority funding.

Residential care (for social reasons) is not provided free of charge in England and Wales (unless you have a relatively low amount of savings and low income). This section briefly outlines the extent to which you may have to contribute to your care, and the implications of this.

Whether or not you pay is determined by your income and savings. There is a fixed Upper Limit to the amount of savings you can have and still receive local authority funding towards the cost. This limit is usually adjusted upwards in April each year.

Currently (2012/13) the Upper Limit is £23,250 in both England and Wales. If you have savings in excess of this amounts you will have to pay the full cost of your care until such time as your savings fall to the Limit when the local authority will start to part contribute.

Your home

If you own your own home its value will be counted as 'capital' and part of your savings. This usually means that you will be expected to sell it to pay the fees. However, your home will not be counted as capital, and therefore not have to be sold if your spouse (or partner) lives in the house, or a close relative under the age of 16 or over the age of 60 (or a relative of any age who is incapacitated) needs to go on living there.

Sometimes the local authority may also ignore the value of the house if it is the permanent home of someone like a carer. This is at the discretion of the local authority.

In all other circumstances you will have to sell your home to realise its value to pay for the care fees. The only exception to this is that, if you do not wish to sell your house, the authority *may* allow you to defer payment of your contribution, to be paid in full when the house is eventually sold (in effect granting you an interest-free loan).

Calculating your Contribution

If your savings (including the value of your home) amount to more than £23,250 you will be liable to pay all the care fees, regardless of your income.

If and when your savings fall below (or equal) this Upper Limit the local authority will step in and make a contribution to the fees. Both your savings and your income will be taken into account when calculating the contribution.

So far as your savings are concerned there is a Lower Limit which, like the Upper Limit, is adjusted upward each April. Currently the Lower Limit in England is £14,250.

Any savings below the Lower Limit are ignored for calculation purposes. For each £250 (or part thereof) of savings you have above the Lower Limit you are deemed to receive an income of £1 per week.

So, for example, if you are living in England and have savings totaling £14,600 your notional income will be £2 per week. To this notional income is added all your other income from pensions (state, occupational or personal) and any income from benefits, to arrive at a figure for your total weekly income.

When deciding on the level of contribution you must make towards your care fees the local authority must always leave you with some spending money. This is called a Personal Expenses Allowance. Currently (2012/13) this is set at £23.50 per week in England (£24.00 in Wales) and is adjusted every April.

Subtracting your Personal Expenses Allowance from your total weekly income gives the level of contribution the local authority will require from you to cover your care costs, up to the full amount of the fees.

Illustrative Example (financial year 2012/13)

Suppose a person in residential care in England has savings of £15,600, state pension of £103 per week and a small private pension of £25 per week. What contribution to their care home fees will they have to make?

Their notional income from savings is calculated as follows - £15,600 less the lower limit of £14250 is £1350. 1350 divided by 250 is 5.4. Therefore the notional income from savings is £6 per week (the figure is always rounded up)

Contribution calculation;

		£
Notional Savings		6.00
State Pension	103.00	
Private Pension	25.00	128.00
Total weekly income		134.00
Less Personal Allowance		23.50
Required Weekly Contribution		110.50

Any shortfall between your contribution and the actual care home fees is paid by the local authority.

In Wales there is no Lower Limit and therefore no calculation of notional income to be included when assessing the level of income. Apart from that there is no difference in the system of assessment in Wales, except that the Personal Allowance in Wales is £24.00, not £23.50 as in England.

Giving away property and savings

Note that it is illegal to give property or savings to another person in order to qualify for financial help from your local authority. Such actions are referred to as Deprivation of Assets and if the local authority suspects that this has occurred they may try to reclaim the fees.

If you give away your home you may lose control over what happens to it. Even though you may feel protected if you give it to your children or other family members you may have no legal rights if things change.

N.B. The above is a brief and simplified explanation of the means of calculating an individual's contribution to the costs of residential care, when needed for social reasons, in England and in Wales. The figures stated are subject to change during the course of a year and, in any event, change every April. The bases for charges for residential care for health reasons are calculated differently and supervised by the NHS, not the local authority.

4. Funding a Funeral

The cost of funerals has risen inexorably over the past several years and the trend shows no sign of abating.

A recent (2012) survey published by Sun Life Direct showed that the cost of funerals in the UK had risen by an average of 71% since 2004. According to the survey the average cost of a funeral in in 2012 was £3284 (excluding costs such as flowers, catering, headstone, death notices, venue hire, etc.). Generally, burials are more expensive than cremations, sometimes markedly so in areas where land is in short supply.

Funeral Bonds

It is possible to pay for one's funeral in advance by purchasing a Funeral Bond (sometimes known as a Funeral Plan). This has the advantage of letting you purchase at today's prices so that you beat any future inflationary rise.

Your pre-payment is guaranteed and ring-fenced in a trust fund.

Bonds are offered by most of the large funeral directors in the UK but you should shop around and check which aspects are guaranteed not to incur additional charges, as there is some variation. Usually prices are only guaranteed for cremations, due to the continuing shortage of burial grounds.

Most bonds offer a choice of funeral type, from simple through to elaborate. It is also possible to plan a bespoke funeral (i.e. draw up a funeral directive) and fund it with a bond. There is no limit on age. Anyone over 18 can purchase a bond on their own or on another's behalf. The age of the nominated person is not limited in any way and no medical examination is required, or indeed any information other than the name and gender of the nominee.

With some providers of bonds it is also possible to pay by instalments. If death occurs before the final instalment has been paid the funeral will be carried out as specified, and the balance due paid out of the proceeds of the estate.

Alternative Funding

Usually the costs of the funeral will be charged against, and ultimately paid by, your estate. If you purchased a bond the cost will, of course, have already been paid.

If you are concerned that your estate may not have sufficient funds to cover your funeral expenses, you may want to consider taking out a whole of life or fixed-term assurance policy which will pay out a guaranteed lump sum on your death.

Setting up such an assurance policy to fund the funeral will enable undertakers to be paid promptly (as their terms of business often require) and thereby avoid the problem of waiting for probate to be granted to pay the cost out of the estate.

Such policies are available from leading UK insurance companies and are specifically aimed at those in the age range 50 – 80. Usually no medical examinations or declarations are required and acceptance into the plan is guaranteed.

If you take out such a policy the ultimate usage of the eventual payout is up to you – it does not have to be used to pay funeral expenses and can be used for any purpose.

Part D - Checklist

Your Will

- Have you drawn up a Will?

Reviewing your Will

- When did you draw up your Will?

- When did you last review it?

- Have there been legislative or tax changes in the interim?

- Has your family/circle of friends changed since you wrote your Will?

- Have you changed your mind about your chosen beneficiaries?

- Do you need to review your Will with your solicitor?

Registering your Will

- Have you registered your Will to ensure it will be found after you die?

Organ/Body Donation

- If you would like others to live after your death, have you taken steps to let it be known you would like to donate your organs?

- Do you want to leave your body for research or training purposes? If so, have you made the necessary arrangements?

Lasting Power of Attorney (Personal Welfare)

- Do you want to nominate someone to act on your behalf in terns of your medical treatment and personal welfare should you become mentally or physically incapacitated in the future?

Lasting Power of Attorney (Property & Affairs)

- Do you want to nominate someone to act on your behalf in financial matters if you should become incapable of doing so yourself?

Funeral Directive

- Have you decided whether you want to be buried or cremated, what type of funeral you want, what music should be played or poems read, etc.?

Funding the Funeral

- Have you purchased a bond so the funeral is paid for in advance?

- Have you put aside (or insured for) a sum to pay for your funeral?

Part E - A Final Thought

This book has been written for a simple purpose – to encourage you, the reader, to think about your later years and to contemplate and prepare for the period leading up to the end of your life, and death itself.

The prospect, for most of us, is not a pleasant one. As human beings we have a tendency to push the thought of death aside. We know it will eventually happen, but we prefer to put it to the backs of our minds and not think about it.

However, the consequences of not devoting thought and not taking action will almost certainly be negative, both for ourselves and for our families.

When loved ones die, those who grieve want, indeed deserve, to know how to mark their passing and how to administer and share in any assets left behind. Not to leave clear instructions in these matters can only cause them more grief and worry at best, and perhaps bitter family strife and division at worst.

We live in a time when, compared to previous generations, most of us can look forward to long lives in retirement. For example, life expectancy at birth in the UK for those born in 1980 is now 77.7 years for men and 81.9 years for women (source: Office for National Statistics).

This is good news of course, but with it comes the potential price of failing health and incapacity – about 1 in 5 men can anticipate spending the last period of their lives in some form of residential care, and 1 in 3 women. A significant and growing number of elderly people will suffer some form of mental and/or physical incapacity during their final years.

For our own sakes, if not for others, it is surely prudent to make practical arrangements for such potential occurrences whilst we can, utilising some of the means outlined in this book. By so doing we may improve the quality of the last period of our lives, and at the same time, mitigate the pain, worry, and grief suffered by our family.

Part F - Further Information

Listed here are the names, addresses and contact details of organisations which may offer useful additional information on various aspects of the topics included in this book.

a) Will Registration

Certainty

The Chapel, Chapel Lane, Lapworth, Warwicks, B94 6EU
Tel: 0845 408 0404
Web: www.certainty.co.uk

Certainty offers anyone the opportunity to register their Will, for a modest one-off fee, so that its location can be determined after death.

b) Equity Release

Home Improvement Trust

7 Mansfield Road, Nottingham, NG1 3FB
Tel: 0800 783 7569
Web: www.houseproud.org.uk

The Trust (a not for profit organisation) aims to make equity release schemes more accessible to older people who need to pay for repairs, adaptations and improvements to their homes.

Equity Release Council

Bush House, Aldwych, London, WC2B 4PJ
Tel: 0844 669 7085
Web: www.equityreleasecouncil.com

The ERC is a trade organisation representing the equity release industry. It has succeeded SHIP (Safe Home Improvement Plans) but continues to maintain the latter's code of practice which includes a 'no negative equity guarantee'.

AgeUK

207-221 Pentonville Road, London, N1 9UZ
Tel: 0845 2300 820
Web: www.ageuk.org.uk

AgeUK has been formed by a merger between Age Concern and Help the Aged. The organisation provides help and advice through its website, its advisers and through publications, including advice on equity release schemes.

c) Long-Term Care

NHS Choices

Web: www.nhs.uk/carersdirect
Tel: 0808 802 0202

This NHS website offers comprehensive information on all aspects of Care and Caring, including the difference between Continuing Care which is funded by the NHS and Social Care which is self-funded and local authority supported.

AgeUK

207-221 Pentonville Road, London, N1 9UZ
Tel: 0845 2300 820
Web: www.ageuk.org.uk

AgeUK has been formed by a merger between Age Concern and Help the Aged. The organisation provides help and advice through its website, its advisers and through publications, including advice on residential care.

Elderly Accommodation Counsel (EAC)

89 Albert Embankment, London, SE1 7TP
Tel: 0800 377 70 70
Web: www.eac.org.uk

Elderly Accommodation Counsel (EAC) is a national charity that aims to help older people make informed choices about meeting their housing and care needs. The website contains a wealth of information on the whole topic of residential care and also has a national database of homes.

d) Funeral Planning

National Association of Funeral Directors

618 Warwick Road, Solihull, B91 1AA
Tel: 0845 230 1343
Web: www.nafd.org.uk

A national association of funeral directors who all adhere to a strict code of practice in respect of standards of service, marketing and advertising, price information and estimates. The association offers a pre-paid funeral plan.

National Society of Allied and Independent Funeral Directors

SAIF Business Centre, 3 Bullfields, Sawbridgeworth, CM21 9DB
Tel: 0845 230 6777
Web: www.saif.org.uk

Members operate within a strict code of practice in respect of standards of service - has about 700 members nationwide, mostly small and family firms.

The Natural Death Centre

In the Hill House, Watley Lane, Twyford, Winchester, SO21 1QX
Tel: 01962 712 690
Web: www.naturaldeath.org.uk

This is a charitable project which aims to support those dying at home, and their carers, and to help people arrange inexpensive, family-organised and environmentally-friendly funerals. It offers free information and a number of useful publications.

British Humanist Association

1 Gower Street. London, WC1E 6HD
Tel: 020 7079 3580
Web: www.humanism.org.uk

The BHA maintains a register of officiants who are qualified to perform non-religious funerals. The website contains a search facility to find an officiant in your area.

Marine Consents Team

Marine Management Organisation, Lancaster House, Hampshire Court, Newcastle upon Tyne, NE4 7YH
Tel: 0300 123 1032
Web: www.marinemanagement.org.uk/licensing/marine/activities/burial.htm

If you wish to be buried at sea this is the body to whom application has to be made.

e) Organ/Body Donation

NHS Organ Donor Register

Fox Den Road, Stoke Gifford, Bristol, BS34 8RR
Tel: 0117 975 7575
Web: www.organdonation.nhs.uk

NHS Blood and Transplant (NHSBT) operates the UK Organ Donor Register. The above web site contains lots of useful and interesting information and also offers the facility to 'sign up' online.

The Human Tissue Authority

151 Buckingham Palace Road, Victoria, London, SW1W 9SZ
Tel: 020 7269 1900
Web: www.hta.gov.uk

The HTA is the organisation to whom application must be made for donation of one's body for medical research or training.

f) Lasting Power of Attorney

Office of the Public Guardian

PO Box 15118, Birmingham, B16 6GX
Tel: 300 123 1032
Web: www.publicguardian.gov.uk

The OPG is part of the Department for Constitutional Affairs and acts as the administrative arm of the Court of Protection. The site has a number of downloadable guides and other useful information.

The OPG is the body which is responsible for registering Lasting Powers of Attorney, and it also deals with applications for the appointment of Deputies to administer the affairs of persons who are incapacitated and have not appointed an attorney.

g) General Information

HM Revenue & Customs

IHT & Probate Helpline: 0845 302 0900
Web: www.hmrc.gov.uk

The Law Society

113 Chancery Lane, London, WC2A 1PL
Tel: 020 7242 1222
Web: www.lawsociety.org.uk

Association of British Insurers

51 Gresham Street, London, EC2V 7HQ
Tel: 020 7600 3333
Web: www.abi.org.uk

Appendices

In this section of LifeHolder we include further information and guidance on the topics covered in the previous two sections:

Guide for Executors is written for lay individuals who have agreed to become an executor and is a brief summary of the duties required and responsibilities involved. It describes all the steps and actions required, from registering the death up to the drawing-up of a final account of the estate.

Guide for Donors is written for those who are considering setting up a Lasting Power of Attorney and explains how a Power can be set up, giving one or more attorneys powers to handle their (the donor's) affairs.

Guide for Attorneys is written for lay individuals who may be asked, by a relative or friend, to become their attorney, under a Lasting Power of Attorney, and contains a brief summary of the duties and responsibilities of an attorney so appointed.

Appendix 1 - Guide for Executors

An Executor is responsible for putting into effect the terms and wishes laid out in someone's Will, and winding up their affairs. In brief, an executor is required to:

Register the death, **Arrange** the funeral, **Secure** the home and property of the deceased, **Obtain** a grant of Probate, **Gather** details of all the assets and liabilities of the deceased, **Collect** in, or realise, all the assets of the deceased, **Pay** all debts and expenses attributable to the deceased, **Distribute** the cash and assets from the estate according to the Will, **Transfer** funds remaining which are to be held for children in a Trust to the named trustees and, finally, **Draw** up an account to show how all the financial aspects of the estate have been dealt with

i) Registering a Death
When someone dies, the death needs to be registered within 5 days at the register office in the district where the death has occurred. All large towns have a registry office and some are to be found in smaller conurbations.

Most deaths are registered by a relative of the deceased. The registrar will normally only allow others to register the death (such as someone present at the death, or the person who found the body if death did not occur in hospital) if there are no relatives available to do it.

When registering you will be asked for the following details:

- date and place of death
- name and surname of the deceased, and maiden name if applicable
- date and place of birth
- occupation
- name and occupation of spouse or civil partner, as appropriate
- usual address
- details of any pension or benefits the deceased received from public funds
- date of birth of any surviving spouse or civil partner

The only document you need is the medical certificate of cause of death, issued by the doctor who pronounced the death. If possible you should also take the deceased's NHS medical card.

If the death has been reported to the coroner, the registrar will need additional documentation from them before the death can be registered.

After completing the formalities you will have the opportunity of buying one or more **death certificates**. Almost certainly you will need more than one as each organisation you need to inform of the death (such as the deceased's bank, building society) will require to see a copy.

The registrar will also issue a **certificate for the burial or cremation** of the body. This should be passed to the funeral director since the funeral cannot proceed without it. In cases where a death has been reported to the coroner he or she will normally issue the certificate for burial or cremation.

You will also need to complete a certificate for social security benefits and send this to your local Benefits office so that the Department for Work and Pensions can deal with all matters pertaining to any benefits and state pensions.

ii) Arranging the Funeral

Sometimes the deceased will have expressed their wishes as to the method of disposal of the body (burial or cremation) and their preferences for the funeral service. They may have left informal instructions with a friend or relative or made a more formal statement by completing a Funeral Directive.

Whatever the situation, you will need to consult with family members, particularly any surviving spouse or civil partner, so you are sure that you are acceding to the wishes of the deceased and those of the family.

iii) Securing the home and property of the deceased

If the deceased leaves a surviving spouse, civil partner or other family member living in their home you will not be required to secure it! However, if they lived alone it will be necessary to do so. Until the home is sold, or the lease formally given up, it will be your responsibility to keep it secure.

You will, however, in all cases need to locate and take possession of all relevant documents including bank statements, share certificates, savings account books, cheque books, tax records and indeed everything relating to the financial aspects of the recent life of the deceased.

iv) Obtaining Probate

In order to get authority to deal with the deceased's estate the executor(s) has to obtain a legal document (called a Grant of Representation or Probate) from the Probate Registry, which is part of HM Courts Service. [If no executors are named in the Will, or the person has died intestate, the Grant of Representation is called Letters of Administration.] Without a grant those organisations holding money in the deceased's name (such as banks, building societies, insurance companies etc.) will not be inclined to release the money to you. You cannot sell or transfer a property held in the deceased's sole name without a grant. Having a grant is proof that you may collect the money or sell the property.

As an executor you can apply for probate yourself. The process involves obtaining and completing various forms and completing and returning them to the Probate Registry and to HM Revenue and Customs along with the original Will, an original copy of the death certificate, the necessary fees, and possibly other documents. You must then attend an interview at the Probate Registry.

Not surprisingly most people prefer to appoint a solicitor to apply for the grant on their behalf. It is much simpler and you are not required to attend a personal interview.

v) Write to relevant organisations
The main task at this stage is to ascertain the value of the assets of the deceased, including obtaining valuations of any property or other non-liquid assets. The latter may, of course involve seeking the opinion of experts such as estate agents.

You will also need to ascertain the extent of any liabilities such as utility bills, mortgages or loans.

Given the ability to calculate the net assets you will now be in a position to assess whether any inheritance tax may be due and the likely amounts that beneficiaries will be entitled to receive.

vi) Realise and Collect the Assets and Pay Liabilities and Expenses
Most of the organisations holding money on behalf of the deceased will require to see a copy of the grant of probate and some may also want to see the death certificate.

You will need to set up a separate bank account to receive monies due and to pay liabilities and any expenses such as funeral costs. Specifically, you will need to establish the tax position with HM Revenue and Customs. A payment may be due, or a refund. If the estate was large enough inheritance tax will also be payable.

vii) Distribute cash and assets to beneficiaries
When the final net value after tax has been determined, the money and other assets should be distributed according to the wishes of the deceased as expressed in the Will.

Any legacies should also be paid and any physical assets stipulated in the Will handed over.

viii) Transfer funds in respect of any Trusts

If the Will directed that any trusts be set up, for example for the benefit of any children, the monies should be handed over to the named trustees.

ix) Accounting Record

An account of how the financial aspects of the estate have been dealt with should now be drawn up so that any interested parties may see for themselves how the estate has been distributed.

You may wish, in particular, to send a copy of the account to the major beneficiaries. Note too that HM Revenue and Customs may wish to see a copy.

x) Help and Assistance

Winding up an estate can be a protracted and time consuming process. For this reason most people choose to arrange for professional help and advice.

Appendix 2 -
Guide for Donors

What is A Lasting Power of Attorney?

An LPA is a legal document which enables you (the donor) to nominate another person (an attorney) to deal with your affairs. The attorney should be someone you can trust implicitly. Very often a close relative is chosen, but an attorney can be almost anyone provided they are over the age of 18 and not bankrupt.

Types of LPA

There are two types of LPA. One deals with Property & Affairs (financial matters) and the other deals with Personal Welfare (health and social issues). It is a matter of personal choice whether to draw up a Power of each type, or just one, or neither.

Both are regulated by the Office of the Public Guardian (OPG) a government controlled body and the procedures for establishing them are broadly similar. Each must be made on a statutory form, available from solicitors and legal stationers. Each must be registered by the OPG before the provisions can take effect.

The following paragraphs refer to the Property & Affairs LPA. However, all procedures and descriptions also apply to a Personal Welfare LPA. The one significant difference on the statutory forms is that on the Personal Welfare version you, the donor, are required to state and confirm whether or not you wish to give your attorney(s) the authority to give or refuse consent to life-sustaining treatment on your behalf.

What is the purpose of an LPA?

An LPA is a precautionary step taken by the donor in case he or she considers they may become incapacitated, or otherwise prevented from handling their own affairs, in the future. It literally donates the power to act on your behalf, to the attorney.

An LPA is therefore a very powerful document. As the donor you can donate general powers, giving control over your financial affairs and empowering the attorney to act generally on your behalf and in your interests. In other circumstances you may choose to donate a specific power or powers, for example, to pay your bills but not to sell your assets.

Often a general power may be given with restrictions – for example, power to deal with all your property and affairs but not allowing the sale of real estate or other specific assets.

As donor it is for you to decide, perhaps with the benefit of advice from family and professional advisers, what powers you wish to donate, and in what circumstances.

Is it safe to make an LPA?

As stated above LPAs are very powerful documents. Remember that the person you appoint as your attorney may have complete power over your money, savings, investments and property. If you become mentally incapable, you will be unable to check what they are doing.

When choosing your attorney, consider how well they handle their own financial affairs, whether you can trust them to act in your best interests, and whether they will use your money to provide for your needs.

Safeguards

As a safeguard you can appoint more than one attorney (see below). You can also add conditions to the LPA when you make it, for example, requiring the attorney to make regular reports to your solicitor or your accountant.

There are also safeguards included in the procedures for establishing an LPA. A pre-condition is that you must discuss your intent to set up a Power with someone you know (but excluding your spouse, any relatives or carers, or your chosen attorney – in short anyone who could potentially benefit from a situation where you give a power of attorney).

If you do not know any suitable individual personally you may choose a solicitor, or other professional person. The person you choose to discuss the matter with has then to sign a document called "Statement of certificate provider" confirming that, in their opinion, you are aware of the purpose of the LPA and that no undue pressure is being put on you to create the Power.

You can also nominate, on the statutory form, up to five people to be notified when an application is made to register the Power with the Public Guardian. This is a safeguard since any of these people named will have an opportunity to object to the registration of the LPA

Joint Attorneys

It is possible to appoint more than one attorney. This can be as a safeguard but sometimes joint attorneys are appointed because the donor wants, as well as a close relative or friend, a professional person such as an accountant or a solicitor, to ensure the duties are carried out correctly and efficiently.

Attorneys may be joint, or joint and several. Appointing joint attorneys means that all decisions and actions taken have to be taken jointly (for example, all their signatures will be required on cheques). This can be inconvenient and, if one attorney cannot act for some reason, or dies, the power will fail.

Appointing attorneys jointly and severally means they can act separately or together. This is clearly more flexible. If the donor wishes, restrictions can be imposed (for example, by requiring that all attorneys have to sign for transactions worth over £1000).

Can attorneys charge for their services?

Non-professional attorneys are not expected to charge for their services, although they may be reimbursed (at your option) for reasonable expenses.

Professional attorneys such as solicitors, accountants or banks are entitled to charge.

Registering the LPA

By law your LPA must be registered with the Public Guardian before you lose the mental capacity to make decisions for yourself. Until it is registered the Power cannot be used. Your nominees (noted on the statutory form) will be contacted by the Guardian when registration is requested. If any object to the registration the Guardian will investigate the circumstances and then make a ruling.

It takes at least 35 days from the date of application before the LPA is registered, to allow time for any objections. Once registration is approved, the LPA will be sealed on every page by the Public Guardian and returned to the attorney. From then on the attorney must answer to the Court of Protection if anyone questions their actions and the LPA cannot be ended without the agreement of the Court or the OPG.

The institutions with whom the attorney will have to deal (such as bank, building society, nursing home, Benefits Agency, HM Revenue & Customs etc.) will require sight of the registered document before they will act on the attorney's instructions.

Duties & Responsibilities of an Attorney

The appointed attorney is bound to act in the best interests of the donor and consider their needs and wishes. He/she must not take advantage of the donor's situation to gain any benefit for themselves and they must keep your money and property separate from their own.

Can they make gifts?
An attorney has limited power to make gifts. For example, they can make seasonal gifts (e.g. at Christmas) to people to whom you might normally have made gifts. They can also make gifts, to appropriate recipients, on anniversaries such as birthdays. Or, they could make donations to any charity you might have been expected to support.

If they want to make larger gifts of money or property they must apply to the Court for permission.

Must they keep accounts?

Yes, they have a duty to keep accounts of all their dealings for the donor. They should keep a full record of all the donor's income and expenditure, together with receipts, invoices and bank statements. The Court of Protection can ask that they produce accounts at any time.

Can they sell the donor's house?

Yes, if they feel this is in the donor's best interests and provided there are no restrictions in the LPA which prevent this. They must be confident there is no reasonable chance the donor will be able to return to live at home.

The approval of the OPG or the Court is not required unless the attorney wants to buy the property themselves, or if they want to give it to someone else, or if the sale is below market value.

Can they stop acting as attorney?

Yes. Stopping to act as an attorney is known as "disclaiming the power". They should ask solicitors to prepare a Deed of Disclaimer.

If they are the sole attorney the usual step is for someone to apply to the Court to appoint a deputy. If there are joint attorneys and one wants to give up, the LPA can no longer be used and the donor's affairs will have to be managed in another way. If there are joint and several attorneys the remaining attorney(s) can continue to act under the LPA but the PGO should be informed about the change.

What are the powers of the Court of Protection?

The Court has powers to intervene in running a registered LPA if anyone suspects the attorney is not acting in the donor's best interests. It may also ask them to produce accounts, answer for any dealings, provide documents or information, or explain why they took certain actions. Ultimately the Court has power to suspend or end their duties.

Appendix 3 -
Guide for Attorneys

What is A Lasting Power of Attorney?

An LPA is a legal document nominating one or more attorneys to deal with the affairs of another person (known as a donor). The attorney(s) is chosen by the donor as someone they can trust implicitly and very often it is a close relative. They can, however, be almost anyone provided they are over the age of 18 and not bankrupt at the time they sign.

What is the purpose of an LPA?

An LPA is a precautionary step taken by the donor in case he or she considers they may be mentally incapacitated in the future, or otherwise prevented from handling their own affairs. It literally donates their power to act on their own behalf, to you as an attorney.

An LPA can therefore be a very powerful document. The donor will decide, perhaps with the benefit of advice from family and professional advisers, what powers they wish to donate, and in what circumstances. You need to decide whether you wish to accept the responsibility of becoming an attorney.

Types of LPA

There are two types of LPA. One deals with Property and Affairs (general financial issues) and the other deals with Personal Welfare (health and social issues).

If you are appointed an attorney under an LPA which deals with the donor's Property and Affairs you may be called on to act for them and on their behalf to organise their finances, pay their bills, even perhaps to sell their property.

Sometimes the donor will donate general powers, giving you control over their financial affairs and empowering you to act generally on their behalf and in their interests. In other circumstances the donor may donate a specific power or powers, for example, to pay their bills but not to sell their assets.

If you are appointed an attorney under an LPA which deals with the donor's Personal Welfare you may be required to take decisions about their future healthcare, living arrangements, even to decide on whether or not to give or refuse consent to life-sustaining treatment on their behalf.

The donor may choose to give you general powers or they may elect to impose restrictions or conditions.

Joint Attorneys

Sometimes the donor will appoint more than one attorney. This can be as a safeguard, because an LPA can be a very powerful tool as has been noted. Sometimes it is because the donor wants, as well as a close relative or friend, a professional person such as an accountant or a solicitor, to ensure the duties can be carried out correctly and efficiently.

Attorneys may be joint, or joint and several. If you are appointed jointly with one or more others all decisions will have to be taken jointly (for example, all your signatures will be required on cheques). This can become inconvenient and, if one attorney cannot act for some reason, or dies, the power will fail. If you are appointed jointly and severally you can act separately or together with your fellow attorney(s). This is more flexible. The donor may, if they wish, impose restrictions on you (for example, by requiring that all have to sign for transactions worth over £1000).

Can you charge for your services?

Non-professional attorneys are not expected to charge for their services, although they should be reimbursed for reasonable expenses. Professional attorneys such as solicitors, accountants or banks are entitled to charge.

Registering the LPA

An LPA (of either type) must be registered before it can take effect. Registration is completed by the Office of the Public Guardian (OPG) to whom application must be made.

In most cases the donor will have nominated other individuals (up to five) whom they wish to be advised that registration has been applied for. This is to allow any of them to object to the registration if they so wish. If any objection is made the situation will be resolved by the Court of Protection.

In the case of a Property & Affairs LPA, you will have no powers to act in relation to the donor's affairs when the application has been made and whilst it is being processed. You will have full powers (as determined by the document signed by the donor) once the LPA is registered. It will take at least 35 days from the date of application before the LPA is registered to allow time for any objections, unless the donor has not nominated anyone to be informed, in which case registration will proceed within a few days. In practice, the total time for registration is significantly longer.

In the case of a Personal Welfare LPA the power cannot be used before registration and then only if the donor cannot make the required decision for themselves. The same procedure for hearing possible objections will also prevail.

Once registration is approved, the LPA will be sealed on each page with a Court of Protection stamp and returned to you. After registration you must answer to the Court of Protection if anyone questions your actions.

Many of the institutions with whom you will have to deal on the donor's behalf (such as their bank, building society, nursing homes, Benefits Agency, HM Revenue & Customs etc.) will require sight of the sealed document before they will act on your instructions.

Duties & Responsibilities of an Attorney (Property & Affairs)

As the appointed attorney you are bound to act in the best interests of the donor and consider their needs and wishes. You must not take advantage of the donor's situation to gain any benefit for yourself and you should keep the donor's money and property separate from your own. You are now managing someone else's money and have legal duties which you must respect.

Can I make gifts?
You have limited power to make gifts. For example you can make seasonal gifts (e.g. at Christmas) to people to whom the donor might normally have made gifts. You can also make gifts, to appropriate recipients, on anniversaries such as birthdays. Or, you could make donations to any charity the donor might have been expected to support.

If you want to make larger gifts of money or property, perhaps as part of Inheritance Tax Planning, you must apply to the Court for permission.

Should I keep accounts?
Yes, you have a duty to keep accounts of all your dealings for the donor, which you must be able to produce at any time. You should keep a full record of all the donor's income and expenditure, together with receipts, invoices and bank statements.

The Court of Protection can ask that you produce accounts at any time.

Can I sell the donor's house?
Yes, if you feel this is in the donor's best interests and provided there are no restrictions in the LPA which prevent this. You must be confident there is no reasonable chance the donor will be able to return to live at home.

You do not need the approval of the OPG or the Court unless you want to buy the property yourself, or you want to give it to someone else or the sale is below market value.

Duties & Responsibilities of an Attorney (Personal Welfare)

Your duties are to act on the donor's behalf in matters pertaining to their health and general well-being.

Your duties may be general and without proscribed limit in this regard, including making decisions on life-sustaining treatment, or they may be subject to restrictions or conditions, depending on what the donor has stipulated.

Can I stop acting as attorney?

Yes. Stopping to act as an attorney is known as "disclaiming the power". If the LPA is registered you should ask a solicitor to prepare a Deed of Disclaimer. If you are the only attorney the usual step is for someone to apply to the Court to appoint a receiver.

If there are joint attorneys and one wants to give up, the LPA can no longer be used and the donor's affairs will have to be managed in another way.

If there are joint and several attorneys the remaining attorney(s) can continue to act under the LPA but the OPG should be informed about the change.

It is not possible to add extra attorneys to a registered LPA.

Where can I get further advice?

If you need advice on practical, financial or legal matters, you should get help from us, as solicitors, or other professional or financial advisers. The OPG will advise if your advisers suggest they should be consulted.

What are the powers of the Court of Protection?

The Court has powers to intervene in running a registered LPA if anyone suspects you are not acting in the donor's best interests. It may also ask you to produce accounts, answer for your dealings, provide documents or information, or explain why you took certain actions. Ultimately the Court has power to suspend or end your duties.

What happens when the donor dies?

The LPA automatically ceases on the donor's death. You should send the original LPA and the death certificate to the OPG as soon as possible. The donor's estate should now be dealt with as per the Will, or the rules of intestacy if there is no Will

Notes